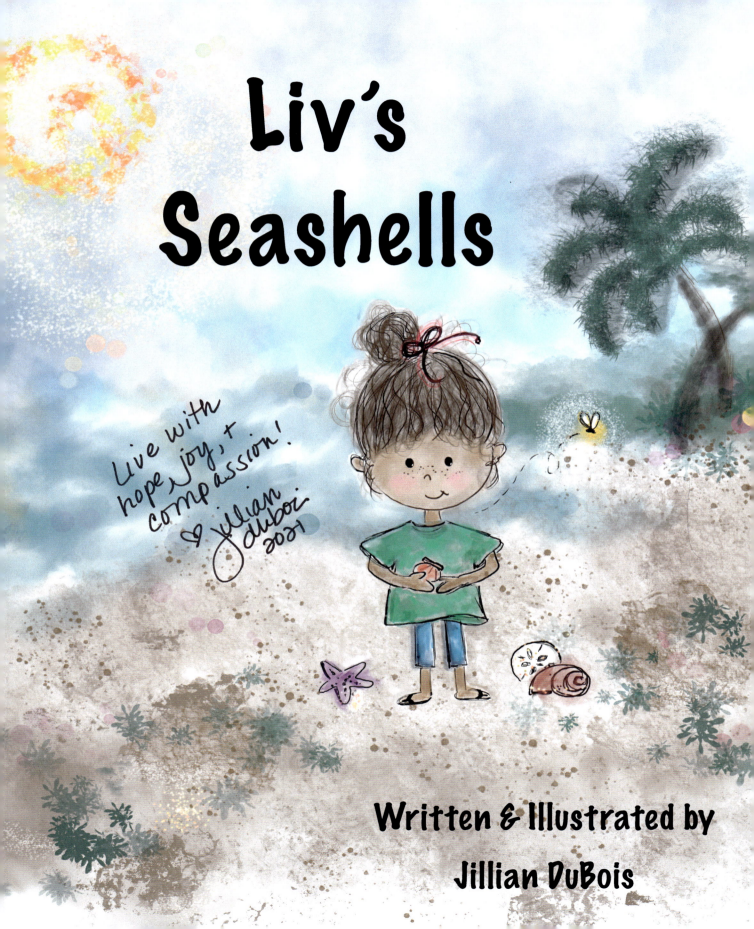

Liv's Seashells

Copyright © by Jillian DuBois

Second Edition 2021

All rights reserved.

No part of this publication may be reproduced in any form, or by any means, electronic or mechanical, including photocopying, recording, or any information browsing, storage, or retrieval system, without permission from the publisher.

Dedicated to my loves, Tim + Austin, who bring me hope and joy each day and encourage me to chase my dreams.

Liv loves the seashore.

The sounds, the smells, and the views of the ocean beckon her to come out and play with a salty welcome.

Liv's bare feet, sandy toes, and sun-kissed rosy cheeks make her heart delighted as she cheerfully runs toward the waves.

Every calming breath, every peaceful moment seems to give her life.

The misty air gives her a burst of energy as she explores along the seashore, curious to find today's treasures.

Liv has the ability to find the most delicate objects that peek ever-so-slightly from beneath the surf and the sparkling sand.

What does she find today?

Seashells.

She is on the watchful hunt today in the tropical breeze.

Big, small, multicolored, unusual, and...

broken.

Yes, broken seashells.

Liv makes two piles of the seashells she finds on the beach.

The first pile is perfect.

They are beautiful, shiny, and stunning to the eye with no flaws.

She holds them in her tiny hand.

But without a doubt, the second pile is her favorite.

Liv delicately searches for the broken seashells and gently lays them down.

She is captivated by the number of them that she has picked up.

She discovers that a variety of them are chipped, cracked, worn, and have lost their colorful sheen.

Liv joyfully takes notice of their charm.

They do not look ruined to her. She only sees the beauty.

Liv has an understanding spot in her heart for the seashells that she saves.

She believes they could benefit from her loving attention.

She squeezes her eyes shut and wishes she could hear their unique stories and tell them all of her own life's secrets.

Sweetly, she brushes off the grains of sand and rinses them carefully under the cool water.

She gently dries her shells and places them in the basket to display on her nightstand.

Liv crawls into bed and glances over to admire the new arrangement of little blessings next to her.

In the stillness of the summer evening, she barely whispers words of comfort and devotion in her small, airy voice...

"I love you just the way you are.

You are not damaged or broken.

I see you as one-of-a-kind.

You are a special masterpiece."

"Each one with a different
size, color, and shape
with imperfections
that make you
amazing and extraordinary."

"Don't let anyone
take away your chance
to sparkle and shine
for what you really are."

Liv turns off the light with a smile and a twinkle in her eye as she says goodnight to her small treasures that have brought her contentment.

As she drifts off to sleep, Liv will be dreaming of what her next adventure could bring as she continues to search the shore for more friends...

She is ever-hopeful to find new opportunities to share heartfelt compassion, positive that there are more for her to cherish.

Dear Readers,

This story was inspired and written as a tribute to my sister, Lisa. She was my Liv in REAL life.

My sister had a heart of compassion and empathy for those around her who needed a friend. Who needed to feel loved and aced.

She sought out those who were different, had brokenness and imperfections. She picked them up where they were to include them in her life. She was generous with her comforting and encouraging words.

It was never important for her to be well-liked, but her purpose was to have genuine love and understanding for others. Lisa was always able to let go of others' expectations of who they thought she should be and was just herself...with joy.

So, this leads me to be able to share this message with the world.

On each illustrated page, be sure to look for a tiny firefly. It is a heartfelt reminder that Lisa's spirit is always with me, lighting up even the darkest spaces when I need it.

Not a day goes by that I don't think of my sister's gracious love and genuine compassion for others. Friends, family, and anyone who met her could confirm her character of acceptance and kindheartedness.

I hope you fall in love with her, too.

Love,

Jillian

Jillian's journey continues to bring much JOY and fulfillment as she thrives on building authentic relationships with her students and guiding their curiosity and wonder. She uses her voice to foster hope for student equity and empathy.

Her passion is to initiate, instill, and infuse joy to those in education through focusing her efforts on listening and growing alongside colleagues and friends.

Jillian personally spends her free time outdoors, soaking up the sun and surf on local Florida beaches, and finding new paths to hike with her husband, son, and black lab.

This is Jillian's first published work as an author and illustrator.

Connect with Jillian at www.impartedjoy.com.

Made in the USA
Monee, IL
21 April 2021